M000092953

CLASS LEADERS

RECOVERING A TRADITION

A LEADER'S GUIDE

By Steven W. Manskar

DISCIPLESHIP RESOURCES

P O BOX 340003 • NASHVILLE, TN 37203-0003
www.discipleshipresources.org

ISBNs

Print   978-0-88177-649-2
epub   978-0-88177-650-8
mobi   978-0-88177-651-5

Grateful acknowledgment is made to Wipf and Stock Publishers for permission to publish this leader's guide. https://wipfandstock.com

Scripture quotations not otherwise indicated are from the New Revised Standard Version Bible © 1989, Division of Christian Education of the National Council of the Churches of Christ in the United States of America. Used by permission. All rights reserved.

Excerpts designated BCP are from the Book of Common Prayer.

Quotations designated *UMBW* are from *The United Methodist Book of Worship*. Copyright © 1992 The United Methodist Publishing House. Used by permission.

Quotations designated *BOD* are from *The Book of Discipline of The United Methodist Church—2012*. Copyright © 2012 The United Methodist Publishing House. Used by permission.

Quotations designated *UMH* are from *The United Methodist Hymnal*. Copyright © 1989 The United Methodist Publishing House.

Class Leaders: Recovering a Tradition, Leader's Guide. Copyright © 2013 Discipleship Resources. All rights reserved. No part of this book may be reproduced in any form whatsoever, print or electronic, without written permission, except in the case of brief quotations embodied in critical articles or reviews and those pages designated reproducible. For information regarding rights and permissions, contact Discipleship Resources, PO Box 340003, Nashville, TN 37203-0003.

Printed in the United States of America

DR 649

To the Instructor

Prerequisite for this course is the Lay Servant Ministries core course *Becoming Accountable Disciples*. Consultation with one's pastor is required before assuming the role of class leader.

This course is intended to equip certified lay servants who have consulted with their pastor and agree that the role of class leader is appropriate within their congregation. **It is important that you remind participants throughout this course that before they attempt introducing class leaders within their congregation, they should have covenant discipleship groups that have been active for at least two years.**

There is a letter to course participants in the addendum of this resource. Please make sure participants have a copy prior to the first session. Materials needed for each session are listed at the beginning of that session.

You are encouraged to invite class participants to lead the opening devotion, "Dwelling in the Word," for sessions two through five. The devotions for these sessions can be found in the addendum of this book.

CONTENTS

THOUGHTS ON TEACHING AND LEARNING

Each of us has a personal and unique learning style. It may be similar to that of others, but if we are able to use a learning style tailored to the way our brain recognizes, stores, and processes information, learning becomes easy and fun, and information is more effectively retained. Think of how you prefer to learn. Perhaps you are a reader. Maybe you learn more easily and efficiently by listening to music, to other sounds, or to someone's voice. Perhaps you learn best in a "hands-on" manner. If the teaching method suits your learning style, you can process and adapt any information quickly. Addressing the educational needs of all students during a session may require you to modify your presentation style.

While lecture alone is the least effective means of presenting material, group activity is one of the most effective. Relational activities in small groups, or sometimes in the larger class context, associate students with different learning styles and thereby offer a way for the teacher to expose students to multiple avenues of learning. Although some sessions will lend themselves to one or more specific learning styles, the instructor can use a combination to address the needs of the students. As teachers, we need to be creative!

Articles and guidelines concerning multiple intelligences refer to the research of Howard Gardner, or the "eight ways of learning." These disciplines can be loosely grouped into three categories or styles: auditory, visual, or tactile (also known as kinesthetic, as it can involve any form of participatory motion or perceived movement). Here are some activity suggestions:

Auditory
Class discussion
Show-and-tell
Creative rhythms and raps
Debate
Paraphrase or description
Music, songs, or rhymes
Poetry, storytelling, and reading
Word games
Seminars

Visual
Charts and graphs
Time lines and diagrams
Cartoons and bulletin boards
Photographs and videos
Posters
Journal writing
Montages, collages, and collections

Tactile
Games and simulations
Puppets
Sculpting
Drama, dance, and role-playing
Singing
Construction
Experiments
Origami and jigsaw puzzles

INTRODUCTION

Class Leader

The title of this course and the office it attempts to illuminate is troublesome. When people hear the term *class leader* they usually assume it describes a Sunday school teacher. Others associate it with leaders of social class. This confusion occurs because most United Methodists have no memory of class leaders serving in the church. The office fell into disfavor and was ignored for decades before the requirement was removed from the *Book of Discipline* in the early twentieth century. Class leaders and class meetings were once important parts of Methodist practice and identity but are now neglected and forgotten.

For the purpose of this course, it is important to understand that class leaders and class meetings were the sinews of Methodism. John Wesley gives the class leader's job description in the General Rules:

> That it may the more easily be discerned whether they are indeed working out their own salvation, each society is divided into smaller companies, called **classes**, according to their respective places of abode. There are about twelve persons in a class, one of whom is styled the **leader**. It is his duty:
>
> 1. To see each person in his class once a week at least, in order: to inquire how their souls prosper; to advise, reprove, comfort or exhort, as occasion may require; to receive what they are willing to give toward the relief of the preachers, church, and poor.

2. To meet the ministers and the stewards of the society once a week, in order: to inform the minister of any that are sick, or of any that walk disorderly and will not be reproved; to pay the stewards what they have received of their several classes in the week preceding (*BOD*, ¶ 104).

The function of the class leader was similar to a coach. Class leaders taught their classes the basic practices and beliefs of Christian discipleship. They also provided the discipline, support, and accountability people needed to apply what they learned to their daily lives. Class leaders provided the frontline pastoral care within the early Methodist societies in Britain and America.

Disciples Make Disciples

Class leaders are the leaders in discipleship every congregation needs. They are the ones best equipped to form others into faithful, dependable disciples of Jesus Christ. A seminary education is not a prerequisite for the work of making disciples. All that is required is "faith working through love" (Gal. 5:6). Class leaders are lay women and men from all walks of life who remember their baptism and center their lives upon Jesus Christ. They renounce the spiritual forces of wickedness; reject the evil powers of this world and repent of their sins; accept the freedom and power God gives to resist evil, injustice, and oppression in whatever forms they present themselves; and confess Jesus Christ as Savior, placing their whole trust in his grace, and promise to serve him as Lord, in union with the church (see "Baptismal Covenant I," *UMH*, 34). Class leaders are members of the congregation who take to heart and act upon the baptismal commendation to "do all in your power to increase their faith, confirm their hope, and perfect them in love" (see "Baptismal Covenant I," *UMH*, 38).

Class Leaders Today

Today, class leaders are women and men who meet weekly with a Covenant Discipleship group. After consultation with the pastor they are commissioned by the congregation (see *BOD*, ¶ 256.16). Class leaders are given pastoral responsibility for up to twenty members of the congregation. This means they help the members of their "class" practice and mature in discipleship shaped by the General Rule of Discipleship: To witness to Jesus Christ in the world and to follow his teachings through acts of compassion, justice, worship, and devotion under the guidance of the Holy Spirit (*Class Leaders*, 70–71).

Class leaders meet with their pastor monthly. These meetings give the pastor an opportunity to support and train class leaders. Class leaders, in turn, help the pastor monitor the pulse of the congregation. The partnership between the pastor and class leaders exists to make certain that the congregation is living out its mission to make disciples of Jesus Christ for the transformation of the world.

Class Leaders: Recovering a Tradition by David Lowes Watson is the main text for this course and is available from Cokesbury.

This course will explore the origins of the office of class leader in the Wesleyan Methodist tradition. It examines the need for recovering the lay pastoral ministry of the class leader for the twenty-first-century church. Participants will see how the ministry of the certified lay servant intersects with that of the class leader.

THE NEED FOR LEADERS IN DISCIPLESHIP

Materials
- Bibles
- *The United Methodist Hymnal* (*UMH*)
- Chalkboard/dry-erase board/newsprint
- Paper/pens/markers

Learning Goals

Students will explore the difference between church membership and discipleship. They will explore Jesus' relationship with people who came to him in need of healing, reconciliation, and out of curiosity, and those who chose to follow him and pattern their lives after his. Students will see that the life of discipleship includes discipling others.

Dwelling in the Word (30 minutes)

Prayer

Almighty God,
> whose Son our Savior Jesus Christ is the light of the world:

Grant that your people,
> illumined by your Word and Sacraments,
> may shine with the radiance of Christ's glory,
> that he may be known, worshiped, and obeyed
> > to the ends of the earth;

through Jesus Christ our Lord,

who with you and the Holy Spirit lives and reigns,
one God, now and for ever. *Amen.* (BCP, 215)

Scripture: Matthew 5:13-16

Reflection (10 minutes)

Instruct participants to partner with a person whom they do not know well.

Each person has three minutes to respond to the question, *What captured your imagination in the scripture reading?*

Listen carefully because each person will be invited to share briefly with the group what his or her partner had to say. It is okay to take notes.

Allow six minutes for the pairs to share with each other. Signal to the group when three minutes has passed and it is time for the other person to share. At the end of the six minutes, bring the conversation to a close and invite persons to share briefly with the class what they heard their partner say.

After everyone has spoken, invite the class to discuss together what God is up to in this passage for the church today.

Invite the class to respond in "popcorn" fashion. You may want to note a summary of each comment on a chalk/whiteboard.

Hymn, "Jesus, United by Thy Grace," UMH, no. 561 (stanzas 1–3)

The Twofold Ministry of Jesus (30 minutes)

We are looking at what David Lowes Watson calls "The twofold ministry of Jesus" (*Class Leaders*, 5). In this section, Watson argues that Jesus extended compassion and healing to everyone he encountered. Watson cites several instances in the Gospels in which people come to Jesus for a variety of reasons. He accepts and loves them as they are. Jesus gives himself freely to all who are in need.

Form groups of three. Assign each group one of the following passages of scripture.

- Matthew 9:32-38
- Matthew 14:34-36
- Mark 10:13-16
- Mark 2:1-12
- Luke 8:43-48
- Luke 9:10-17
- John 10:1-6
- John 5:2-9
- John 12:44-50

Instruct participants to read their assigned passage, paraphrase it, and discuss the following questions:

- What does Jesus do?
- What does Jesus expect or demand of the person(s)?
- What does this story tell us about Jesus?

We see in the Gospels that while Jesus loved and accepted everyone, he wanted his disciples to know what following him would demand of them. Discipleship is a commitment of a person's entire self to following Jesus and striving to become like him. In the following passages we look at the ways Jesus helped potential disciples count the cost of discipleship.

In the same groups of three, assign each group one of the passages below.

- Matthew 10:34-39
- Matthew 16:24-26
- Mark 8:34-38
- Luke 9:23-27
- Luke 9:57-62
- Luke 14:25-33
- John 13:12-17
- John 15:1-17
- John 15:18-27

Instruct participants to read their assigned passage, paraphrase it, and discuss the following questions:

- What does Jesus do and say?
- What does Jesus expect or demand of the person(s)?
- What does this story tell us about living as a disciple of Jesus Christ?

A Disciple's Job Description (30 minutes)

David Lowes Watson writes, "Jesus also impressed upon his disciples that they were not superior to other people. On the contrary, they were to make themselves everyone else's servant" (*Class Leaders*, 6).

In the Gospels, Jesus' disciples enjoy his company. They are blessed by their relationship with him. However, Jesus clearly teaches that the benefits of discipleship come with responsibilities. Following and learning from him equips the disciples to be his witnesses in the world and to follow his teachings through acts of compassion, justice, worship, and devotion. Discipleship is a life given to service with Christ in the world.

We will now consider the character and responsibility of discipleship. Form groups of four. Give each group a sheet of paper and a pen, pencil, or marker. Instruct participants to write a job description (see addendum) of a disciple based upon the four passages of scripture listed below. (15 minutes)

- Matthew 14:13-21
- Mark 10:35-45
- Luke 10:1-12
- John 21:15-17

Invite the groups to share their job descriptions with the class. Discuss what the job descriptions have in common and where they differ.

Discuss (15 minutes)
- How does your congregation define what constitutes a disciple?
- What is your congregation's job description for a disciple of Jesus Christ?

- How does your congregation equip members to become and serve as disciples of Jesus Christ?

Class Leaders: Disciples Who Make Disciples (30 Minutes)

When Jesus calls people to be disciples, he calls them to a life of obedience and service. David Lowes Watson writes, "Our costly commitment is not for our own benefit, but for the sake of Christ—and everyone in Christ's family. Our sole privilege is that of servanthood" (*Class Leaders*, 22).

As disciples habitually obey Jesus' commands to love God with all their heart, soul, and mind and love those whom God loves (Matt. 22:34-40), they become disciples who disciple others. Christians who answer the call to accountable discipleship will always be a minority in the church. The church needs accountable disciples to live out its mission with Christ in the world. They serve as role models, mentors, coaches, and helpers.

In the Wesleyan Methodist tradition, "class leader" is the historic title given to leaders in discipleship. The class meeting was the small group all Methodists were required to join. The class consisted of twelve to fifteen men and women who met for one and a half hours a week. The class leader was a mature follower of Jesus Christ in whom others recognized trustworthiness for the care of souls. He (or she) led the weekly meeting that consisted of prayer, hymn singing, Bible study, and accountability for discipleship. Methodists learned how to live as Christians in the world from the care and example of their class leader.

Invite the class to gather in pairs and respond to the following questions. (10 minutes)

- Who are the people in your congregation doing work similar to that of the class leader?
- What are some of the ways they serve?
- How is the work of class leaders similar to the work of Lay Servants?
- Do you see yourself serving as a class leader? Why or why not?

Invite each pair to share their responses with the class. Then ask the question, *How would class meetings and class leaders change the church today?*

Closing and Dismissal

Assignment: Read the introduction and chapters 1–4 in *Class Leaders: Recovering a Tradition* in preparation for the next class.

Ask a volunteer to lead the opening devotion for the next class. Devotions for sessions two through five can be found in the addendum of this resource.

Hymn, "Jesus, United by Thy Grace," *UMH*, no. 561, stanzas 4–6

Invite participants to share prayer concerns, and then offer a closing prayer.

RECOVERING THE TRADITION OF CLASS LEADERS

Materials
- Bibles
- *The United Methodist Hymnal* (*UMH*)
- Copies of "A United Methodist Rule of Life" (addendum)
- Newsprint
- Markers
- Tape

Learning Goals
Students will explore the meaning of tradition and the office of class leader. They will then look at the General Rules (A United Methodist Rule of Life), the General Rule of Discipleship, Covenant Discipleship, and the contemporary office of class leader.

Dwelling in the Word (30 minutes)

Prayer
Almighty God,
> whose Son our Savior Jesus Christ is the light of the world:
Grant that your people,
> illumined by your Word and Sacraments,
> may shine with the radiance of Christ's glory,
> that he may be known, worshiped, and obeyed
>> to the ends of the earth;

through Jesus Christ our Lord,
who with you and the Holy Spirit lives and reigns,
one God, now and for ever. *Amen.* (BCP, 215)

Scripture: Matthew 5:43-48

Reflection (10 minutes)

Instruct participants to partner with a person whom they do not know well.

Each person has three minutes to respond to the question, *What captured your imagination in the scripture reading?*

Listen carefully because each person will be invited to share briefly with the group what his or her partner had to say. It is okay to take notes.

Allow six minutes for the pairs to share with each other. Signal to the group when three minutes has passed and it is time for the other person to share. At the end of the six minutes, bring the conversation to a close and invite persons to share briefly with the class what they heard their partner say.

After everyone has spoken, invite the class to discuss together what God is up to in this passage for the church today.

Invite the class to respond in "popcorn" fashion. You may want to note a summary of each comment on a chalk/whiteboard.

Hymn, "A Charge to Keep I Have," *UMH*, no. 413

Tradition (35 minutes)

Tradition is the act of handing down a custom from one generation to the next. For Christians, tradition is how the gospel *of* Jesus and the gospel *about* Jesus are handed down from one generation to another. Too often tradition is equated with the trappings and practices of an institution. Tradition is sometimes used by people seeking to resist change by clinging to practices, beliefs, and places long past. Tradition, when properly understood and practiced, is how the church remains centered in Christ "to serve the present age" in language, symbols, and practices the church understands (see stanza 2 of "A Charge to Keep I Have," *UMH*, no. 413).

Jesus summarizes the gospel in Mark 1:15 saying, "The time is fulfilled, and the kingdom of God has come near; repent, and believe in the good news."

Jesus came into the world to proclaim the reality of God's kingdom. He lived and preached the message of God's rule of righteousness and justice breaking into the world. God's shalom is a present reality and a promised hope. Jesus describes his mission in Luke 4:18-19. The Sermon on the Mount (Matt. 5-7) gives his followers a glimpse of life in the reign of God. The two great commandments (Matt. 22:34-40, Mark 12:28-34, and Luke 10:25-28) are Jesus' summary of how we are to live in God's reign.

Related to the gospel *of* Jesus Christ is the gospel *about* Jesus Christ, summarized in Acts 10:34-43. Jesus is the incarnation of God's love for the world (John 3:16). Sins are forgiven. Relationship with God, neighbors, and self are restored. In Jesus, God provides the grace we need to realize God's acceptance and live as children of God's household (2 Cor. 5:16-21).

Tradition entails practices and teaching that enable the church to build and sustain a community that faithfully witnesses to Jesus Christ in the world. Over the course of several years of pastoral experience, John and Charles Wesley established several traditions among the people called Methodist. These traditions helped sustain the Methodists, who were both missional and evangelical. The primary purpose of these traditions was to keep the Methodist societies centered on Jesus Christ, his teachings, and his mission.

Field preaching, the love feast, the covenant service, the General Rules, class meetings, and class leaders are all part of the Methodist tradition.

Ask class members to pair off and respond to the following question:

• What are the essential traditions of your congregation?

After five minutes, ask the pairs to discuss this question:

• What are the essential traditions of The United Methodist Church?

Allow five minutes for the groups to reflect on the question and then bring the class together and invite participants to share the essential traditions of their respective congregations. Write these traditions on a sheet of newsprint. Next, invite the group to share what it believes to be essential Methodist traditions. Compare the two lists and then ask the following questions:

- How do the traditions listed "tradition" the gospel *of* Jesus Christ?
- How do the traditions listed "tradition" the gospel *about* Jesus Christ?

Methodist practices were designed to *tradition* the gospel in the hearts and lives of the Methodist people. *Traditioning* forms holy habits that shape the character of women and men who profess faith in the triune God and seek to grow in love of God and neighbor by following Jesus Christ in the world.

In her book *Soulfeast: An Invitation to the Christian Spiritual Life*, Marjorie Thompson writes, "A rule of life is a pattern of spiritual disciplines that provides structure and direction for growth in holiness. . . . It fosters gifts of the Spirit in personal life and human community, helping to form us into the persons God intends us to be." In 1743, John Wesley developed the Methodist rule of life known as "The General Rules" (see "The United Methodist Rule of Life" in the addendum). They are summarized here:

> It is therefore expected of all who continue therein that they should continue to evidence their desire of salvation,
>
> *First*, by doing no harm by avoiding evil of every kind, especially that which is generally practiced.
>
> *Secondly*, by doing good; by being in every kind merciful after their power; as they have opportunity, doing good of every possible sort, and, as far as possible, to all [people].
>
> *Thirdly*, by attending to all the ordinances of God; such are: the public worship of God; the ministry of the Word, either read or expounded; the Supper of the Lord; family and private prayer; searching the Scriptures; fasting or abstinence (*BOD*, ¶ 104).

The purpose of these basic practices is to equip the congregation to participate in Christ's mission in the world by obeying his teachings contained in Matthew 22:37-40:

> He said to him, "'You shall love the Lord your God with all your heart, and with all your soul, and with all your mind.' This is the greatest and first commandment. And a second is like it: 'You shall love your neighbor as yourself.' On these two commandments hang all the law and the prophets."

The General Rules established a pattern of life that traditioned the gospel throughout the Methodist societies across Britain and America.

In the same pairs, instruct the class to respond to the following questions. (10 Minutes)

- How does your congregation teach the General Rules?
- What is your congregation's rule of life?
- How does your congregation's "rule of life" compare to the General Rules?

Traditioning the Gospel Requires Balance (30 minutes)

In Matthew 22:37-40, Jesus encapsulates the shape of life in the kingdom of God now and in the age to come. He shows us that life in God's reign is cross-shaped. Loving God with all your heart, soul, and mind is the vertical axis of life in God's reign. Loving your neighbor as yourself is the horizontal axis. Loving God and loving those whom God loves is the cross Jesus tells his followers to take up, and they are able to take it up as long as they follow him (Luke 9:23-25).

John Wesley called the practices that helped people come to know and love God "works of piety." He called the practices of loving our neighbor "works of mercy." He termed works of piety and works of mercy "means of grace." They are means of grace for at least two reasons. First, Jesus taught and practiced them throughout his life and embodied life in the reign of God. He expected his followers to follow his lead (see John 14:16-17). Second, they open our hearts to the presence and power of God in the world through Jesus Christ and the Holy Spirit. The works of mercy and piety are where God promises to meet us and where we make ourselves available to him and his love.

In groups of four, look at "A United Methodist Rule of Life" then discuss the questions below.

(10 minutes)

The General Rules are intended to help Christians maintain balance in their discipleship. They are a simple, explicit guide to practices that are supported by scripture and tradition. Rules one and two give direction in how to love your neighbor as yourself. Rule three lists the practices that direct the heart, soul, and mind toward loving God.

Instruct participants to look at the first General Rule: "By doing no harm, by avoiding evil of every kind . . ." and notice the list of behaviors John Wesley provides as examples of actions Methodists ought not do. Then ask the following questions:

- Which of these do you think are no longer applicable to today? Why?
- What would you add to this list?

(10 minutes)

Instruct participants to look at the second General Rule: "By doing good; by being in every kind merciful after their power; as they have opportunity, doing good of very possible sort, and, as far as possible to all [people]. . ." and then ask the following questions:

- Why are works of mercy essential to discipleship (see Matt. 25:31-46 and Luke 10:25-37)?
- What are some examples of works of mercy?
- How are you doing no harm?
- How are you doing good?

(10 minutes)

Instruct participants to look at the third General Rule: "By attending upon all the ordinances of God. . ." The list Wesley provides here are the practices he called "works of piety." Piety is "habitual reverence and obedience to God." These are the basic practices God gives to open the heart, soul, and mind to the power of grace. As you look at the list you will notice the balance Wesley provides between social acts of worship (the public worship of God, the ministry of the Word, and the Supper of the Lord) and the personal acts of devotion (family and private prayer, searching the scriptures, and fasting or abstinence).

Wesley knew that piety awakens and empowers mercy. When the heart, soul, and mind are habitually opened to God, the Holy Spirit redirects them from self-centeredness to Christ-centeredness. To be Christ-centered is to be alongside the poor and vulnerable people of the world (Matthew 25:40). Ask the class the following questions:

- Why are works of piety essential to discipleship?
- How does your congregation teach and equip members to habitually practice works of piety?
- What do you think of the following assertion: Leaders in discipleship are women and men who habitually practice the General Rules (or The United Methodist Rule of Life) and lead others in doing likewise.

Summary (5 minutes)

In this session we have looked at tradition and its importance to discipleship and leadership. We have discussed the meaning of tradition as practices by which the church teaches the gospel to each generation. We can say that tradition is both a noun and a verb. We must always be mindful that tradition does not exist for its own sake. Its sole purpose is the gospel. Like the church, tradition must never exist for itself.

A rule of life is a tradition that helps keep traditions and mission centered in Jesus Christ and his gospel. It provides a set of basic practices that each generation learns and habituates in order to build community, form character, and go out in mission to the world.

Class leaders are men and women who know, teach, and practice the church's traditions. They are the leaders who help convey the gospel of Jesus Christ from one generation to the next.

In session three, we will look closely at a contemporary version of the General Rules known as the General Rule of Discipleship and how it helps form leaders who practice and teach the way of Jesus. We will also examine the balance between works of mercy and works of piety.

Closing and Dismissal

Assignment: Read chapter 4 in *Class Leaders: Recovering a Tradition.*

Ask a volunteer to lead the opening devotion for the next session. Devotions for sessions two through five can be found in the addendum.

Hymn, "Jesus, Thine All Victorious Love," *UMH*, no. 442, verses 1–4

Invite participants to share prayer concerns, and then offer a closing prayer.

THE GENERAL RULE OF DISCIPLESHIP

Materials
- Bibles
- *The United Methodist Hymnal* (*UMH*)
- Copies of "The General Rule of Discipleship" (addendum)
- Newsprint
- Markers
- Tape

Learning Goals
The primary task of a class leader is to help Christians grow in discipleship shaped by the General Rule of Discipleship. This session will familiarize participants with the General Rule of Discipleship. We will explore its role in disciple formation in the congregation.

Dwelling in the Word (30 minutes)

Prayer
O God, the strength of all who put their trust in you:
Mercifully accept our prayers;
    and because in our weakness we can do nothing good
        without you,
    give us the help of your grace,
    that in keeping your commandments
        we may please you both in will and deed;

through Jesus Christ our Lord,
> who lives and reigns with you and the Holy Spirit,
> one God, for ever and ever. *Amen.* (BCP, 216)

Scripture: Matthew 22:34-40

Reflection (10 minutes)

Instruct participants to partner with a person whom they do not know well.

Each person has three minutes to respond to the question, *What captured your imagination in the scripture reading?*

Listen carefully because each person will be invited to share briefly with the group what their partner had to say. It is okay to take notes.

Allow six minutes for the pairs to share with each other. Signal to the group when three minutes has passed and it is time for the other person to share. At the end of the six minutes, bring the conversation to a close and invite persons to share briefly with the class what they heard their partner say.

After everyone has spoken, invite the class to discuss together what God is up to in this passage for the church today.

Invite the class to respond in "popcorn" fashion. You may want to note a summary of each comment on a chalk/whiteboard.

Hymn, "Let Us Plead for Faith Alone," *UMH*, no. 385

The General Rule of Discipleship (30 minutes)

In session two we looked in detail at the General Rules of The United Methodist Church. In this session we will explore a contemporary adaptation of the General Rules known as the General Rule of Discipleship: To witness to Jesus Christ in the world and to follow his teachings through acts of compassion, justice, worship, and devotion under the guidance of the Holy Spirit.

Dr. David Lowes Watson developed this rule to serve as the foundation for a small-group ministry he modeled after the Methodist Class Meeting. The General Rule of Discipleship helps Christians practice the General Rules in their daily lives.

The General Rule of Discipleship is to a disciple what scales are to a musician. Disciples of Jesus Christ are much like musicians. Disciples must practice the basics of Christian faith and life for the same reason a musician needs to practice each day. Discipleship begins with God's love and the Christian's desire to grow in holiness of heart and life. Growth requires disciplined practice of the basics: works of mercy and works of piety. Discipline and practice frees the Christian to live as a witness to Jesus Christ for the world. The General Rule of Discipleship guides disciples in practices that become holy habits.

Ask any musicians in the class to raise their hands. Invite them to talk about how practice helps maintain and improve their ability to perform.

In groups of three, discuss the questions below. (5 minutes)

- What would happen if you became more disciplined in practicing works of mercy and works of piety?
- How would becoming more intentional about practicing the General Rule of Discipleship change you?

Two Great Commandments

When asked what the greatest commandment is Jesus responded,

> "'You shall love the Lord your God with all your heart, and with all your soul, and with all your mind.' This is the greatest and first commandment. And a second is like it: 'You shall love your neighbor as yourself.' On these two commandments hang all the law and the prophets" (Matt. 22:37-40).

These two great commandments are applied through a General Rule of Discipleship: To witness to Jesus Christ in the world and to follow his teachings through acts of compassion, justice, worship, and devotion under the guidance of the Holy Spirit.

In the same groups of three discuss the question below. (5 minutes)

- How does the General Rule of Discipleship complement the General Rules?

Balanced Discipleship

The importance of the General Rule of Discipleship is the balance it maintains among all of Jesus' teachings:

Personal
- ◆ Acts of Devotion
- ◆ Acts of Compassion

Public
- ◆ Acts of Worship
- ◆ Acts of Justice

Works of Piety: Loving God with all your heart, soul, and mind
- ◆ Acts of Worship
- ◆ Acts of Devotion

Works of Mercy: Loving your neighbor as yourself
- ◆ Acts of Compassion
- ◆ Acts of Justice

Acts of Compassion are simple acts of kindness we do for our neighbor. Our neighbor is anyone who is in need, anywhere in the world.

Acts of Justice are how we not only minister to people in need, but also ask why they are in need. In the name of Christ, we must address the social and institutional causes of our neighbor's suffering.

Acts of Worship are the means of grace in word and sacrament that we exercise together. They enable us to build each other up as members in the body of Christ (see 1 Corinthians 12:12-31).

Acts of Devotion are the private spiritual disciplines of prayer, Bible reading, fasting, and inward examination that bring us face-to-face with God.

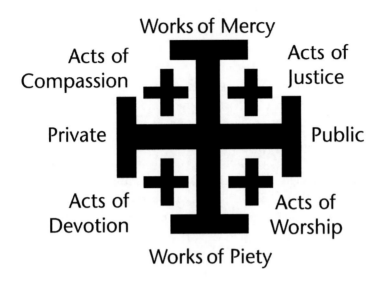

Works of Mercy

Acts of Compassion

Acts of Justice

Private

Public

Acts of Devotion

Acts of Worship

Works of Piety

In groups of three, brainstorm examples of acts of compassion, justice, worship, and devotion. Instruct the group to select a scribe to record the group's work. Allow ten minutes for this exercise. Invite each group to present its work to the class.

A General Rule (10 minutes)

Read or paraphrase the following information to the class, and then invite the class to respond.

The General Rule of Discipleship is precisely what the name implies: a *general* rule. It is not meant to be followed to the letter, simply because each disciple is a unique person, with his or her own temperament, gifts, and skills. You will quickly discover this in your congregation, where each member will prove to have distinctive strengths and skills. You will find this is true in the various vocations that motivate each person.

These distinctive gifts and graces should be used to the fullest, not least of all because they will complement and enhance the strengths and skills of each person in the congregation. The New Testament image of

the body of Christ is helpful in this regard: Each part of the body con-
tributes to the well-being of the whole because each part is distinct yet
inseparable. So it is with discipleship. Each of us has a unique contribution
to make to the whole.

The General Rule of Discipleship is not prescriptive. It does not tell
you what to do. You are free to discern how to practice acts of compassion,
justice, worship, and devotion. It is directive, like lines on a piece of paper
or a compass. It keeps you in the way of Jesus.

The General Rule of Discipleship is inclusive and liberating. New
Christians and seasoned disciples find a place within its bounds. It pro-
vides the discipline that frees Christians to live and love the way of Jesus.
As discipline and practice frees a musician to perform with confidence, the
General Rule of Discipleship frees Christians to become the persons God
created them to be.

Say to the group: Practicing scales, chord changes, and songs frees a
person to perform music to the best of his or her ability. The General Rule
of Discipleship provides an outline for the disciplined practice of Christian faith and life that frees Christians to become fully the persons God
created them to be in the image of Christ.

Ask the group, *Do you agree with the statement:* The purpose of discipline is freedom. *Why or why not?*

"To witness to Jesus Christ in the world. . . ."
(10 minutes)

A witness testifies to the truth, often by the content of his or her life and
character. A witness to Jesus Christ reveals the truth of Jesus' proclamation: "The time is fulfilled and the kingdom of God has come near; repent
and believe in the good news" (Mark 1:15).

In groups of three, invite participants to discuss different ways of act-
ing as witnesses to Jesus Christ in the world. What does it look like to
witness to Christ in the world? Give examples of where you see God's
reign active in the world today. For examples of what the reign of God
looks like read Matthew 5:3-11; Mark 6:30-44; Luke 7:22-23. Allow seven
minutes for discussion and then invite each group to share its reflections
with the class.

"... and follow his teachings through acts of compassion ..." (10 minutes)

An act of compassion allows us to enter into the suffering of our neighbor. Our neighbor is a person anywhere in the world who is hungry, thirsty, lonely, vulnerable, sick, or imprisoned (Matt. 25:34-40). Acts of compassion are works of mercy and kindness we extend to persons in need. They are personal and often private.

In the same groups of three, invite the class to discuss the following question:

• What acts of compassion are you willing to practice and be accountable for each week?

"... and follow his teachings through acts of ... justice ..." (10 minutes)

In his book, *Covenant Discipleship: Christian Formation through Mutual Accountability*, David Lowes Watson writes, "We must not only minister to people in need, but also ask why they are in need. In the name of Christ, we must implement God's righteousness and denounce injustice."

Justice is an attribute of God's holiness. The God of justice seeks the well-being of all people. Justice insists that all persons have access to everything needed to live and become the persons God created us to be. Justice leads to shalom, God's vision for the world.

Justice is the social consequence of compassion. Where acts of compassion alleviate the suffering of individuals, acts of justice address the systems and institutions responsible for suffering. The following story illustrates the difference between acts of compassion and acts of justice.

The people living in a small, rural town must travel fifty miles to the nearest city when they need medical care. This is a great hardship for the elderly and poor residents who either do not own a car or cannot drive. A small group of people from one of the churches in town makes themselves available to drive people to see a doctor in the city.

One day a group of people in the church organized a meeting with church and community leaders to discuss ways to bring a medical clinic to their town. After many meetings and consultation with county and state leaders and the hospital in the neighboring city, a clinic was opened in the small town. People no longer needed to travel fifty miles to receive care.

The people who made themselves available to drive their neighbors to the doctor practiced acts of compassion. Their love of God revealed in Jesus Christ compelled them to love their neighbor as themselves by giving of their time to drive the elderly and poor fifty miles to receive medical care.

The same people participated in acts of justice when they worked with the church and community efforts to organize and bring a medical clinic to their town. They helped to address the cause of their neighbors' fear of lack of access to adequate health care.

Draw a vertical line down the center of a sheet of newsprint. At the top of the left-hand column write "Acts of Compassion." At the top of the right-hand column write, "Acts of Justice." List the following under "Acts of Compassion:"

"I was hungry and you gave me food,"
"I was thirsty and you gave me something to drink,"
"I was a stranger and you welcomed me,"
"I was naked and you gave me clothing,"
"I was sick and you took care of me,"
"I was in prison and you visited me."
(Matt. 25:35-40)

Form groups of four. Instruct each group to discuss and identify one act of justice that addresses each of the issues Jesus names in Matthew 25. Allow five to seven minutes for discussion and then invite each group to report its work to the class. Ask participants to share with their groups what acts of justice they would be willing to practice and be accountable for in a small group of other disciples each week.

". . . and follow his teachings through acts of . . . worship . . ." (20 minutes)

Read aloud or paraphrase the following:

Acts of worship are the public and social dimension of works of piety. They are the way Christians in community express their love for God through prayer, praise, confession, proclamation, and sacraments. Worship is the Christian's response to God who has given himself to us through the life, death, and resurrection of his Son (John 3:16). We offer ourselves in worship to God through ritual. Worship opens our hearts to God and his grace when we gather in his name to offer ourselves in service to his mission in the world.

Three of the six works of piety that John Wesley lists in the third General Rule are acts of worship:

The public worship of God

> On Sunday mornings the church gathers in the name of the triune God to honor and serve him in praise, proclamation, thanksgiving, and sacrament.

The ministry of the word, either read or expounded

> When Christians gather in the name of Christ the word is read and expounded. The gospel of Jesus Christ is proclaimed as the good news to those who hear it. The reading and interpretation of scripture is a means of grace.

The Supper of the Lord

> John and Charles Wesley believed the Lord's Supper is a converting and sustaining means of grace. John Wesley thought it of such importance that he included it alongside prayer and searching the scriptures in his sermon, "The Means of Grace." He wrote another sermon entitled, "The Duty of Constant Communion," in which he argued that Christians should receive the sacrament weekly, and more frequently when possible. Charles Wesley wrote a collection of 166 hymns on the Lord's Supper. John and Charles Wesley believed Methodists should take seriously Jesus' command to "Do this in remembrance of me" (Luke 22:19).

Public worship and the Lord's Supper are essential to the life and mission of the church. The ministry of the word, while part of public worship, may also be practiced in informal small-group settings.

In addition to the public means of grace, John Wesley introduced the love feast and covenant service to the Methodists. Due to their intimate nature, these rituals were reserved for members of the Methodist societies and not open to the public. Wesley adopted the love feast from the Moravians. It is an informal service of praise, singing, prayer, and testimony, led by laypersons, during which bread and water are shared and an offering collected for the relief of the poor. A contemporary order for the love feast can be found in *The United Methodist Book of Worship*, 581–584.

John Wesley adapted the covenant service for the Methodists in 1755. On or near New Year's Day, Methodists gathered for this solemn service of covenant renewal. It is a powerful way to begin a new year. A contemporary version of the covenant service can be found in *The United Methodist Book of Worship*, 288. In groups of four, discuss the following quotation by John Wesley:

> Is not the eating of that bread, and the drinking of that cup, the outward, visible means whereby God conveys into our souls all that spiritual grace, that righteousness, and peace, and joy in the Holy Ghost, which were purchased by the body of Christ once broken and the blood of Christ once shed for us? Let all, therefore, who truly desire the grace of God, eat of that bread and drink of that cup (Sermon 16: "The Means of Grace," § III.12).

The Lord's Supper has been at the center of Christian worship from the early days of the church. For John and Charles Wesley, the sacrament was central to both worship and the formation of Christian character.

- Would you participate in the Lord's Supper more frequently if it were offered? Why or why not?
- What acts of worship are you willing to practice regularly and be held accountable for each week?

". . . and follow his teachings through acts of . . . devotion . . ." (10 minutes)

Acts of devotion are the personal means of grace we practice privately. These daily acts nurture our personal relationship with God who comes to us in Jesus Christ and the Holy Spirit. John Wesley defined "means of grace" as the "outward signs, words, or actions ordained of God, and appointed for this end—to be the ordinary channels whereby he might convey to [people] preventing, justifying, or sanctifying grace" (Sermon 16: "The Means of Grace," §II.1). Three of the "ordinances of God" Wesley lists in the third General Rule are acts of devotion:

- Family and private prayer
- Searching the scriptures
- Fasting or abstinence

While there are other spiritual disciplines Methodists could practice, Wesley thought these three to be particularly important since they were taught and practiced by Jesus himself. Personal prayer, Bible study, and fasting open our hearts to Christ and keep us with him. They are like the relationship skills we engage in with a spouse, lover, or friend. Prayer is like conversation with our beloved. We open our hearts and lives to the beloved and listen as she or he shares her or his life, hopes, and dreams with us. In prayer, we tell Christ what is on our heart and mind, and then we listen for what he has to say in response. Bible study is akin to the ways we learn our beloved's life story. When we read, study, and pray with scripture, we learn about Jesus, his way of living and loving, and we find our life in his. Finally, fasting is a powerful form of self-denial. When we love another person, our needs and wants become secondary to the needs and wants of our beloved. This enables us to participate more fully in our beloved's life. In the process, we take on some of the character of our beloved. Fasting from food is an ancient Christian practice of self-emptying. When we refrain from eating for a day, or part of a day, we imitate the self-emptying of God Paul writes about in Philippians 2:7. Charles Wesley describes this beautifully in the third stanza of the hymn "And Can It Be that I Should Gain" (*UMH*, no. 363):

He left his Father's throne above
(so free, so infinite his grace!)
emptied himself of all but love,
and bled for Adam's helpless race.
'Tis mercy all, immense and free,
for O my God, it found out me!

When Christians empty themselves in fasting they allow God to fill them with his love through prayer. Fasting is closely linked to prayer and scripture. The inevitable hunger pangs and physical discomfort that accompany fasting is a physical prompt to feast on God's word in scripture and reflect upon God's grace in prayer.

Fasting is also a means of remembering the people with whom Jesus most closely identified himself—the poor (see Matthew 25:31-46). Jesus calls his followers to serve and be advocates and friends of the countless poor of the world, many of whom live with hunger as a constant companion.

John Wesley said this about the importance of prayer:

And first, all who desire the grace of God are to wait for it in the way of prayer. This is the express direction of our Lord himself. In his Sermon upon the Mount, after explaining at large wherein religion consists, and describing the main branches of it, he adds: 'Ask, and it will be given to you; search, and you will find; knock, and the door will be opened for you. For everyone who asks receives, and everyone who searches finds, and for everyone who knocks, the door will be opened.' (Matthew 7:7-8). Here we are in the plainest manner directed to ask in order to, or as a means of, receiving; to seek in order to find the grace of God, the pearl of great price (Matthew 13:46); and to knock, to continue asking and seeking, if we would enter into his kingdom (Sermon 16: "The Means of Grace," §III.1).

In the same groups of four, discuss the following question:

- How would you teach a person who is preparing for baptism to pray?

John Wesley said this about searching the scriptures:

Secondly, all who desire the grace of God are to wait for it in 'searching the Scriptures'. Our Lord's direction with regard to the use of this means is likewise plain and clear. 'Search the Scriptures', he says to the unbelieving Jews, 'for they testify of me' (John 5:39). And for this very end did he direct them to search the Scriptures, that they might believe in him (Sermon 16: "The Means of Grace," §III.7).

Discuss the following question:

- How would you teach a person preparing for baptism to read and study scripture?

Conclude this section by asking the class to reflect on the following question:

- What acts of devotion are you willing to practice regularly and be held accountable for each week?

". . . under the guidance of the Holy Spirit." (10 minutes)

Read aloud or paraphrase the following:

Discipleship and leadership are the work of the Holy Spirit in the church. The Holy Spirit is working in the world, in the church, and in human beings to prepare this world for the coming reign of God "on earth as it is in heaven" (Matt. 6:10). The Spirit opens hearts, minds, eyes, and ears to recognize the places where God's reign is breaking out in the world each day. As people, communities, and institutions recognize the presence of the kingdom in their midst, their priorities and behavior are reoriented toward God's promised reign. They know it is coming because the Holy Spirit gives them the awareness of its presence, both big and small, around them everyday.

When a congregation is guided by the Holy Spirit it becomes an outpost of the kingdom of God in a broken and hurting world. An outpost is like an embassy that represents the values and customs of a nation. If you visit the embassy of the Republic of South Africa in Washington, D.C., you are actually on South African territory. In crossing the threshold of the embassy you leave the United States and enter South Africa. At the embassy you will experience the best of South African culture and hospitality. When "persons visit our worship services, sample our programs, or merely come on to our premises, they should quickly sense in whose name and for the sake of whose gospel we are gathered" (David Lowes Watson, *Forming Christian Disciples*, 37).

Class leaders are women and men guided by the Holy Spirit. They are persons who have the "form and the power of religion" in their lives. Class leaders are leaders in discipleship who habitually practice the means of grace in order to grow in holiness of heart and life. They lead in discipleship by virtue of their witness among their peers in the congregation and their service in the world. Their status as leaders in discipleship comes from their openness to the guidance of the Holy Spirit who provides the grace needed to obey the teachings of Jesus Christ to both love God and those whom God loves (Matt. 22:37-40).

The central task of the class leader is to extend the General Rule of Discipleship into the life and practice of the congregation. Class leaders are disciples who help form other disciples within their congregation. They work as partners in ministry and mission with the appointed pastor, sharing in the pastoral ministry of the church to make disciples of Jesus Christ to participate in Christ's mission of preparing the world for the coming reign of God.

Form groups of four and invite the groups to discuss the following question:

- How is your congregation an outpost of the kingdom of God for its visitors, neighbors, and community?

Closing and Dismissal

Assignment: Read chapter 5 in *Class Leaders: Recovering a Tradition*.

Ask a volunteer to lead the opening devotion for the next class. Devotions for sessions two through five can be found in the addendum.

Hymn, "Christ, from Whom All Blessings Flow," *UMH*, no. 550

Invite participants to share prayer concerns, and then close by offering the following prayer:

O God, you have made of one blood all the peoples of the earth, and sent your blessed Son to preach peace to those who are far off and to those who are near: Grant that people everywhere may seek after you and find you, bring the nations into your fold, pour out your Spirit upon all flesh, and hasten the coming of your kingdom; through Jesus Christ our Lord, who lives and reigns with you and the Holy Spirit, one God, now and for ever, *Amen.* (BCP, Collect for the Mission of the Church)

COVENANT DISCIPLESHIP GROUPS

Materials
- Bibles
- *The United Methodist Hymnal* (*UMH*)
- Copies of "The General Rule of Discipleship," "A Cross-Shaped Life," and the "Sample Covenant" (addendum)
- Covenant Discipleship brochure
- Adhesive notes
- Newsprint
- Markers
- Tape

Learning Goals

Covenant Discipleship groups are essential to the formation of class leaders. This session will introduce participants to Covenant Discipleship groups. They will learn about the character of these groups, how they work, and how to write a covenant. Participants will learn the importance of participation in a weekly covenant discipleship group.

Dwelling in the Word (30 minutes)

Prayer

O Lord, you have taught us
that without love whatever we do is worth nothing:

Send your Holy Spirit and pour into our hearts your greatest gift,
  which is love,
    the true bond of peace and of all virtue,
      without which whoever lives is accounted dead before you.
Grant this for the sake of your only Son Jesus Christ,
  who lives and reigns with you and the Holy Spirit,
    one God, now and forever. *Amen.* (BCP, 216)

Scripture: 1 John 3:11-22

Reflection (10 minutes)

Instruct participants to partner with a person whom they do not know well.

Each person has three minutes to respond to the question, *What captured your imagination in the scripture reading?*

Listen carefully because each person will be invited to share briefly with the group what his or her partner had to say. It is okay to take notes.

Allow six minutes for the pairs to share with each other. Signal to the group when three minutes has passed and it is time for the other person to share. At the end of the six minutes, bring the conversation to a close and invite persons to share briefly with the class what they heard their partner say.

After everyone has spoken, invite the class to discuss together what God is up to in this passage for the church today.

Invite the class to respond in "popcorn" fashion. You may want to note a summary of each comment on a chalk/whiteboard.

Hymn, "Love Divine, All Loves Excelling," *UMH*, no. 384

The Class Meeting for Today (5 minutes)

Familiarize yourself with this introduction and present it to the class in your own words.

Historically, the class meeting was the heart of Methodism. Most Methodists received the gift of faith in Christ in these weekly meetings of twelve to fifteen women and men. The class meeting taught Methodists how to pray and read the Bible. The pastoral care and guidance of the class leader provided the accountability and support the people needed to live as witnesses to Jesus Christ in the world. Until the late nineteenth century, all Methodists were required to meet weekly with their class and class leader.

The class meeting was an incubator of the lay leadership that carried out the mission and ministry of Methodism. Class meetings formed leaders in discipleship. They made disciples who could then go and make disciples themselves. Class meetings and class leaders were essential components of the method of Methodism. They provided the form and connected people to the power of discipleship.

The class meeting and class leaders are a distant memory in the United Methodist Church today. While they continue to function in Black Methodism, they are little more than historic relics to the vast majority of United Methodists.

A version of the class meeting, however, continues today in Covenant Discipleship groups. This ministry was developed by Dr. David Lowes Watson in the mid-1980s. It is an adaptation of the class meeting and emerged from Dr. Watson's research and writing about the early Methodist class meeting. He realized that contemporary congregations provide much of what the class meeting once accomplished—fellowship, Bible study, and prayer groups. Absent from the church today is mutual accountability for discipleship. The Covenant Discipleship group fills this need.

Covenant Discipleship groups are comprised of between five and seven people who agree to meet for one hour each week. Mutual accountability for discipleship is the purpose of the weekly meetings. The discipleship of the group is guided by a covenant written by the members and shaped by the General Rule of Discipleship. Covenant Discipleship groups are designed to form leaders in discipleship who help the local church equip its members to participate in Christ's mission in the world. Some of these individuals will be commissioned by the congregation to serve as class leaders.

This session takes an in-depth look at Covenant Discipleship groups.

Two Great Commandments and the Cross-Shaped Life (10 minutes)

Form groups of five. Distribute copies of "The Cross-Shaped Life" (addendum) to participants, and then invite a member of the class to read Matthew 22:34-40 aloud.

Instruct the class to take five minutes to read the explanation on the second page of "The Cross-Shaped Life." After everyone has had time to read, invite the groups to discuss the following questions:

- Which part of "The Cross-Shaped Life" do you tend to empha-size—the vertical works of piety or the horizontal works of mercy? Why?
- How is your discipleship balanced between works of piety and works of mercy?
- If balance is lacking, how can you practice a more balanced discipleship?

The General Rule of Discipleship (30 minutes)

Jesus summarized his teachings in two great commandments: "'You shall love the Lord your God with all your heart, and with all your soul, and with all your mind.' This is the greatest and first commandment. And a second is like it: 'You shall love your neighbor as yourself.' On these two commandments hang all the law and the prophets" (Matt. 22:37-40).

The Two Great Commandments shape the life and work of Cove-nant Discipleship groups and are applied through the General Rule of Discipleship:

> To witness to Jesus Christ in the world
> and to follow his teachings through acts of
> compassion, justice, worship, and devotion
> under the guidance of the Holy Spirit.

Write the General Rule of Discipleship on a piece of newsprint and post it on a wall in front of the class in a place where it is easily visible. Distribute four adhesive notes to each group. If possible, give each group a different color. On another piece of newsprint draw a large cross that divides the sheet into quadrants. Leave margins around the page.

Write "Works of Mercy" in the middle of the top margin.
Write "Works of Piety" in the middle of the bottom margin.
Write "Personal" in the middle of the left-hand margin.

Write "Social" in the middle of the right-hand margin. Instruct the class to write "Acts of Compassion" on one adhesive note, "Acts of Justice" on another, and likewise with "Acts of Worship" and "Acts of Devotion." Ask participants to discuss with their groups in which quadrant each adhesive note belongs. A representative from each group should then place the adhesive notes in each quadrant. Take a moment to observe the location each group has placed its adhesive notes. Are all of the groups in agreement? If not, where is there disagreement? Invite the groups to give their rationale for the placement of their adhesive notes.

Once each group and/or individual has had an opportunity to explain their decisions, distribute copies of The General Rule of Discipleship (addendum). After everyone has received a copy, give the explanation below of the balanced discipleship contained in the General Rule of Discipleship.

Balanced Discipleship

Familiarize yourself with this introduction and present it to the class in your own words.

The importance of the General Rule of Discipleship is the balance it maintains between all of Jesus' teachings: Loving God with all your heart, soul, and mind is practiced in daily life by loving your neighbor as yourself. If we truly love God, then we must love those whom God loves. Jesus and the writers of the Old and New Testaments taught that loving one's neighbor reveals the depth and character of our love for God. Our neighbor is anyone, anywhere in the world, who is hungry, homeless, sick, blind, oppressed, or outcast. In Matthew 25:31-46, Jesus identifies himself with his neighbor. When we serve our neighbor through works of mercy, we find ourselves in the presence of Christ himself.

Works of mercy and works of piety bring disciples into God's presence. When we spend time with God we naturally grow in holiness of heart and life—we become more and more like what we love.

The Personal (Acts of Devotion and Acts of Compassion) is balanced with the Social (Acts of Worship and Acts of Justice). Works of piety (Acts of Worship and Acts of Devotion) are balanced with works of mercy (Acts of Compassion and Acts of Justice).

The practice of discipleship balanced between works of mercy and works of piety equips Christians to become persons for whom love is their natural response to the world.

Form groups of five. Instruct the groups to take a deep breath and then hold it as long as they are able. When participants can hold their breath no longer, they should exhale until all the breath taken in on the inhale has been exhaled through the lips without taking an additional breath.

Invite the groups to discuss the following questions:

- How did it feel to take in the deep breath and then hold it?
- How did it feel to exhale without taking any air into your lungs?
- How healthy is either behavior if you made a habit of it?

Say to the class: Inhaling and holding our breath is like persons or congregations who emphasize the works of piety while neglecting the importance of works of mercy.

Exhaling all the time is like persons or congregations who emphasize the works of mercy while neglecting the importance of the works of piety. Both behaviors are exhausting and unhealthy. Healthy, Christ-centered discipleship requires a balance of inhaling (piety) and exhaling (mercy). The two are intimately linked.

Definitions

Acts of Compassion: The simple acts of kindness we show our neighbor (anyone who is in need, anywhere in the world).

Acts of Justice: We must not only minister to people in need, but also ask why they are in need. In the name of Christ, we must address the social and institutional causes of our neighbor's suffering.

Acts of Worship: These are the means of grace that we exercise together—the ministries of word and sacrament. They enable us to build each other up in the body of Christ.

Acts of Devotion: These are the private spiritual disciplines of prayer, Bible reading, and inward examination that bring us face-to-face with God.

In the same groups of five, ask each group to brainstorm different acts of compassion, justice, worship, and devotion. Instruct the groups to select one member to serve as the scribe and record the group's ideas. After five minutes, invite the groups to reach a consensus on one act in each of the four categories (5 minutes). The scribes from each group should then go to the newsprint page containing the adhesive notes from the previous exercise and write the acts of compassion, justice, worship, and devotion each group has agreed upon in the appropriate quadrant.

Covenant Discipleship Groups (5–7 minutes)

Review the following information with the class. You may wish to distribute copies of the Covenant Discipleship brochure available from the General Board of Discipleship. The brochure can be obtained by sending requests for brochures to cdgroups@gbod.org.

Covenant Discipleship Groups

A Covenant Discipleship group is five to seven persons who meet together for one hour each week to hold themselves mutually accountable for their discipleship. The group shares a covenant they themselves have written. The group's covenant is shaped by the General Rule of Discipleship. During the weekly meetings the members "watch over one another in love" by giving one another a weekly compass heading. The group is task-oriented, and its goal is to help one another become better, more consistent disciples of Jesus Christ.

Covenant Discipleship groups are a trustworthy and effective means of identifying and nurturing disciples who disciple others. They are not where our discipleship happens but where we make sure it happens.

Covenant Discipleship Group Dynamics

The weekly meeting is a simple process of question and answer that gives the leader a directive role. There is no permanent leader. Members take turns leading each week. The leader opens meetings with prayer and takes the group through the covenant. The leader always begins with himself or herself.

The weekly meetings are one hour each. The covenant is the agenda. This keeps the focus of conversation on discipleship.

Over time the group develops an atmosphere of trust and sharing. It is important that members focus on those aspects of their discipleship that can be helpful to the group. Group members agree to respect the confidentiality of the group; anything shared within the group stays within the group.

The Covenant Discipleship Group Covenant (35 minutes)

Covenant Basics (10 minutes)

Begin with the General Rule of Discipleship. It is the framework upon which the covenant is built.

Start where you are, not where you think you should be. A common mistake made by groups as they begin to write their covenants is that members include acts of compassion, justice, worship, and devotion they think they should be doing, rather than acts they are actually willing and able to do. For example, a group may agree they should emulate John Wesley's practice of prayer and Bible reading for two hours every day, an hour early in the morning and another hour at night. While this is certainly a worthy goal, it is highly unlikely the members of the group will actually pray and read their Bible for two hours every day. A more realistic clause, one that everyone is more likely to practice might say, "We will pray and read our Bible every day."

The covenant is a statement of intent. It points the group members toward a goal. The covenant is not to be used as a means of judgment or a source of guilt. Rather, it is a guide for following Christ throughout the week.

A covenant is a living document of consensus. Everyone in the group must agree to every word on the page before it becomes the group's covenant of discipleship. This means covenant writing is a process of respectful listening and compromise.

The group should revisit and revise the covenant annually. The covenant should be adjusted as the group changes and grows in holiness of heart and life. If a clause becomes routine, then the group may want to find ways to make it more challenging. If a clause is regularly neglected, then it should be replaced by another clause the group is actually willing and able to do.

Three Essential Parts

Preamble

The preamble states the nature and purpose of the covenant. It makes clear the covenant is not a set of regulations, emphasizes the group's dependence upon grace, and is a statement of shared faith in Christ.

Clauses

Clauses must be balanced among acts of compassion, justice, worship, and devotion. It must include at least one clause in each of the four categories. Clauses should appear in the same order as the categories are listed in the General Rule of Discipleship (i.e. acts of compassion, followed by acts of justice, worship, and then devotion). Keep clauses as simple and as specific as possible. Limit clauses to acts everyone is actually willing and able to do. Include at least one clause that acknowledges promptings and warnings of the Holy Spirit. This assures the group will be mindful of the Spirit's activity and respond accordingly. Finally, the covenant should have between eight and ten clauses. Your covenant should fit on one side of a single page.

Conclusion

The conclusion is a brief statement reaffirming the nature and purpose of the covenant. It emphasizes that grace is the dynamic of discipleship.

Points to Note

- Each group writes its own covenant.
- The group may take as long as it needs to write the clauses.
- The covenant should be a statement that each member can affirm in faith and practice.
- The clauses of a covenant should all be practical, both to attempt and to sustain. They can always be changed as the group members grow in their discipleship.
- The clauses should reflect the context of the group. Members should feel free to introduce clauses that respond to particular situations and to change or even drop clauses that are no longer relevant.

Covenant Writing Exercise (25 minutes)

In the same groups of five, distribute copies of the sample covenant found in the addendum, and ask participants to look at the list of acts of compassion, justice, worship, and devotion they brainstormed earlier in the class. Take ten minutes to reach a consensus on one act of compassion, one act of justice, one act of worship, and one act of devotion that each person in the group is willing and able to accomplish. Invite each group member to give a brief account of how he or she plans to practice each and incorporate the acts into his or her life. Discuss how weekly accountability in practicing balanced discipleship helps shape Christians into leaders who disciple others.

Closing and Dismissal (5 minutes)

Assignment: Read chapters 6 and 7 in *Class Leaders: Recovering a Tradition*.

Ask for a volunteer to lead the opening devotion for the next class. Devotions for sessions two through five can be found in the addendum.

Hymn, "A Charge to Keep I Have," *UMH*, no. 413

Invite participants to pray the "Covenant Prayer in the Wesleyan Tradition" (*UMH*, no. 607) as the closing prayer.

The Work of a Class Leader

Materials
- Bibles
- *The United Methodist Hymnal (UMH)*
- Newsprint
- Markers
- Tape

Learning Goals
Participants will develop an understanding of the work of class leader. This session will teach methods for getting to know the class members and ways of encouraging them to grow in discipleship guided by the General Rule of Discipleship.

Dwelling in the Word (30 minutes)

Prayer
O God, you have taught us to keep all your commandments
     by loving you and our neighbor:
Grant us the grace of your Holy Spirit,
     that we may be devoted to you
          with our whole heart,
     and united to one another with pure affection;
through Jesus Christ our Lord,
     who lives and reigns with you and the Holy Spirit,
     one God, for ever and ever. *Amen.* (BCP, 230–231)

Scripture: Ephesians 4:1-16

Reflection (10 minutes)

> Instruct participants to partner with a person whom they do not know well.
>
> Each person has three minutes to respond to the question, *What captured your imagination in the scripture reading?*
>
> Listen carefully because each person will be invited to share briefly with the group what his or her partner had to say. It is okay to take notes.
>
> Allow six minutes for the pairs to share with each other. Signal to the group when three minutes has passed and it is time for the other person to share. At the end of the six minutes, bring the conversation to a close and invite persons to share briefly with the class what they heard their partner say.
>
> After everyone has spoken, invite the class to discuss together what God is up to in this passage for the church today.
>
> Invite the class to respond in "popcorn" fashion. You may want to note a summary of each comment on a chalk/whiteboard.

Hymn, "Jesus, United by Thy Grace," *UMH*, no. 561

Class Leader (30 minutes)

The instructor should read the following lines aloud:

It is the responsibility of class leaders to extend the General Rule of Discipleship throughout the congregation.

Class leaders fill this role by accepting basic pastoral responsibility for *classes* of church members. These classes are not the same as Sunday school classes, nor are they convened as class meetings. They are rather in the nature of pastoral groupings, consisting of fifteen or twenty persons who receive guidance and support from a class leader in living out their discipleship according to the General Rule of Discipleship.

"[Class leaders] provide the class member with help and encouragement in the basics of their discipleship. As the relationship develops, the class leader will become a trusted friend. But the friendship will be a firm one, because it will always be directed toward an accountability for faithful discipleship" (*Class Leaders*, 71–72).

The office of class leader has been absent from the Methodist tradition for over one hundred years. This is why the title sounds strange to twenty-first-century ears. To understand the work of the class leader in contemporary terms, think about coaching. A class leader is very much like a personal coach who walks alongside another person, teaching and modeling a way to live. Like a coach, the class leader encourages and challenges persons on the way towards growth and maturity in faith, what John Wesley called "holiness of heart and life.

Invite class members to return to their conversation partners from the opening devotion. Allow ten minutes (five minutes each) for the pairs to discuss a teacher or coach who has significantly influenced their life. Then ask the class to reflect on the following questions:

- How did he or she help you form good habits?
- How did his or her character and way of living influence you?

Conclude this exercise by reading the following paragraph aloud:

In the Methodist tradition class leaders are the disciples who disciple others. Class leaders are the disciples the church needs to fulfill its mission to make disciples of Jesus Christ for the transformation of the world. They are the coaches who walk alongside members of the congregation who want to grow in discipleship. They serve as role models for discipleship in the church.

Getting to Know Your Class (15 minutes)

Read or paraphrase this section aloud.

Class leaders serve as partners in pastoral ministry with the pastor. The ministry of class leaders is important because the work of Christian formation cannot be the sole responsibility of the appointed pastor(s). In fact, for most of the history of the church lay women and men have served as disciples who disciple others. They are better suited than clergy for the work of disciple-making because their lives are not consumed by the church and its "business."

Pastors are responsible for preaching the gospel, administering the sacraments, and ordering the life of the congregation. The laity—class leaders in particular—are to love and care for one another and do all in their power to increase faith, confirm hope, and perfect one another in love. This is affirmed in the baptismal covenant with these words:

> With God's help we will proclaim the good news and live according to the example of Christ. We will surround these persons with a community of love and forgiveness, that they may grow in their trust of God, and be found faithful in their service to others. We will pray for them, that they may be true disciples who walk in the way that leads to life (the "Baptismal Covenant I," *UMH*, 35).

When a congregation strives to live out the promises made in the Baptismal Covenant it is more likely to become a community in which everyone is known by name. More than knowing everyone by name, members are provided the help and resources needed to be "true disciples who walk in the way that leads to life." This requires leaders who acknowledge the diversity of faith and experience to be present in every congregation.

As they begin their work, it is important for class leaders to understand that they are *not* pastoral counselors. They are discipleship coaches. Their task is to walk alongside the members of the class and help each member grow in holiness of heart and life (loving God and loving those whom God loves), both of which are shaped by the General Rule of Discipleship. Their goal is to form relationships of mutual trust that allow them to help each class member grow in their practice of the basics of discipleship (acts of compassion, justice, worship, and devotion).

In groups of three, invite the class to reflect upon and discuss the following question. (10 Minutes)

- What are the social and cultural pressures that make it difficult for you to be a faithful disciple?

Invite persons to share their responses with the class.

Forming the Discipleship of Your Class (45 minutes)

Once commissioned by the congregation (see *UMBW*, no. 602) class leaders are assigned as many as twenty members of the congregation who desire to grow in discipleship. Class leaders begin their work by building relationships with each of the class members. David Lowes Watson provides helpful guidance for this process in chapter seven of *Class Leaders*, 127–147.

Role-Play Exercise

Ask for six volunteers from the class. Three will play the role of class leader. Three will play the role of new members of a class receiving their class leaders in their homes for the first time.

Allow the pairs three minutes to prepare. The "class leaders" will use the following agenda to guide their introductory meeting with their new class member. They may consult pages 127–131 in *Class Leaders: Recovering a Tradition*. Write the four-point agenda on a sheet of newsprint or whiteboard so it is visible. The "class leader" must cover each of the four points of the agenda:

1. Explain the office of class leader
2. Personal introductions
3. Explain the General Rule of Discipleship
4. Response and discussion

Each pair has ten minutes for the role-play. Allow three minutes of response and discussion from the class between each role-play.

After the role plays are complete, ask the class the following questions:

- What did you learn?
- What would you do differently?
- Why is a clear agenda for the introductory meeting helpful in putting the class member and the class leader at ease?

Closing and Dismissal (10 minutes)

Conclude the class with these words of John Wesley, introduced by David

Lowes Watson in *Class Leaders,* 154:

"Let the last word come from John Wesley himself, whose pastoral instincts allowed the office of class leader to develop in the early societies, as he saw gifts and graces in the lives of men and women called to the task of forming Christian disciples. The words come from a sermon that first appeared in 1787, entitled "The More Excellent Way," and they show how his own leadership of the Methodist movement had tempered his pastoral instincts into a deep wisdom:

> It is the observation of an ancient writer, that there have been from the beginning two orders of Christians. The one lived an innocent life, conforming in all things, not sinful, to the customs and fashions of the world; doing many good works, abstaining from gross evils, and attending the ordinances of God. They endeavoured, in general, to have a conscience void of offence in their behaviour, but did not aim at any particular strictness, being in most things like their neighbours. The other Christians not only abstained from all appearance of evil, were zealous of good works in every kind, and attended all the ordinances of God, but likewise used all diligence to attain the whole mind that was in Christ, and laboured to walk, in every point, as their beloved Master.

"As a class leader, you are this 'other sort of Christian.' You have been called to this 'more excellent way.' But your call is not for your own sake; it is for the sake of others, the members of your class. Lead them well. They are now in your care."

Ask the class, *Do you see yourself serving as a class leader in your congregation? Why or why not?*

Offer a closing prayer, and include the names of those who feel called to the ministry of class leader.

Hymn, "Jesus, Lord, We Look to Thee," *UMH,* no. 562

RECOMMENDED RESOURCES

The following books were written by David Lowes Watson and are available from Cokesbury. They provide the theological, historical, and practical foundations for recovering the Methodist class meeting and class leaders for the twenty-first century. Each of these makes clear the purpose and goal of Covenant Discipleship and the ministry of class leader—making disciples who make disciples. The congregation develops a culture that is centered in Jesus Christ and forms members as his witnesses in the world.

Covenant Discipleship: Christian Formation through Mutual Accountability
(ISBN 1-57910-953-5)

Class Leaders: Recovering a Tradition
(ISBN 1-57910-954-3)

Forming Christian Disciples: The Role of Covenant Discipleship and Class Leaders in the Congregation
(ISBN 1-57910-946-2)

Steven W. Manskar wrote the books listed below.

A Disciple's Journal (Discipleship Resources, published annually). This resource is a guide for daily prayer, Bible reading, and discipleship for Christians striving to grow in holiness of heart and life. Based upon the Revised Common Lectionary, it contains patterns for daily morning and evening prayer, prayers for each day of the week, and excerpts from the works of John and Charles Wesley.

Accountable Discipleship: Living in God's Household (Discipleship Resources, 2003). This resource provides the biblical, theological, and historical foundations for Covenant Discipleship groups and class leaders. This is a good resource for small groups.
(ISBN 978-0-88177-339-2)

A Perfect Love: Understanding John Wesley's 'A Plain Account of Christian Perfection' (Discipleship Resources, 2004). This is a contemporary English translation of John Wesley's defense of his teachings on Christian perfection (also referred to as "entire sanctification" and "Christian maturity"), *A Perfect Love* includes helpful notes, selected stanzas from Charles Wesley's hymns, a leader's guide, and a forty-page theological reflection on Christian Perfection by Dr. Marjorie Suchoki.
(ISBN 978-0-88177-426-9)

For more information on Covenant Discipleship visit
http://www.gbod.org/covenantdiscipleship.

LETTER TO THE COURSE PARTICIPANT

The following letter is to be distributed to course participants prior to the first session.

A prerequisite for taking this course is to have taken the course *Becoming Accountable Disciples*. Consultation with the pastor of your congregation is required before assuming the role of class leader.

Introduction to the Course

Class Leader?

The title of this course and the office it intends to illuminate is troublesome. When people hear the term *class leader* they usually assume it describes a Sunday school teacher. Others associate it with "leaders" of social class. This confusion occurs because most United Methodists have no memory of class leaders serving in the church. This is so because the office had fallen into disfavor and ignored for decades before the requirement was removed from the *Book of Discipline* in the early twentieth century. Class leaders and class meetings were once important parts of Methodist practice and identity but are now neglected and forgotten.

For the purposes of this course, it is important to understand that class leaders and class meetings were the essential sinews of Methodism. John Wesley gives the class leader's job description in the General Rules:

That it may the more easily be discerned whether they are indeed working out their own salvation, each society is divided into smaller companies, called **classes**, according to their respective places of abode. There are about twelve persons in a class, one of whom is styled the **leader**. It is his duty:

1. To see each person in his class once a week at least, in order: to inquire how their souls prosper; to advise, reprove, comfort or exhort, as occasion may require; to receive what they are willing to give toward the relief of the preachers, church, and poor.

2. To meet the ministers and the stewards of the society once a week, in order: to inform the minister of any that are sick, or of any that walk disorderly and will not be reproved; to pay the stewards what they have received of their several classes in the week preceding.

We see here that class leaders functioned very much like a coach on a baseball or football team. They taught their class the basic practices and beliefs of Christian discipleship. They also provided the discipline, support, and accountability people needed to apply what they learned to their daily life. Class leaders provided the frontline pastoral care within the early Methodist societies in Britain and America.

Disciples Make Disciples

Class leaders are the leaders in discipleship every congregation needs. They are the seasoned disciples who are best equipped to form others into faithful, dependable disciples of Jesus Christ. A seminary education is not a prerequisite for the work of disciple making. All that is required is "faith working through love" (Gal. 5:6). Class leaders are lay women and men from all walks of life who remember their baptism and center their lives upon Jesus Christ. They renounce the spiritual forces of wickedness, reject the evil powers of this world and repent of their sins; accept the freedom and power God gives to resist evil, injustice, and oppression in whatever forms they present themselves; and confess Jesus Christ as Savior, put their whole trust in his grace, and promise to serve him as Lord, in union with the church (see "Baptismal Covenant I," *UMH*, 34). Finally, class leaders are members of the congregation who take to heart and act upon the baptismal commendation to "do all in your power to increase their faith, confirm their hope and perfect them in love" (see "Baptismal Covenant I," *UMH*, 38).

Class Leaders Today

Class leaders today are women and men who meet weekly with a Covenant Discipleship group. After consultation with the pastor, they are commissioned by the congregation (see *UMBW*, 602–604). Class leaders are given pastoral responsibility for up to twenty members of the congregation. This means they help the members of their "class" to practice and mature in discipleship shaped by the General Rule of Discipleship: To witness to Jesus Christ in the world and to follow his teachings through acts of compassion, justice, worship, and devotion under the guidance of the Holy Spirit.

Class leaders meet monthly with their pastor. The purpose of these meetings is to provide the pastor an opportunity to provide support and training for the class leaders. The class leaders also help the pastor to take the pulse of the congregation. The partnership between the pastor and class leaders assures that the congregation is living out its mission to make disciples of Jesus Christ for the transformation of the world.

Class Leaders: Recovering a Tradition by David Lowes Watson is the main text for this course and is available from Cokesbury.

This course will explore the origins of the office of class leader in the Wesleyan Methodist tradition. It examines the need for recovering the lay pastoral ministry of the class leader for the twenty-first century church. Participants will see how the ministry of the certified lay servant intersects with that of the class leader.

Copyright © 2013 by Discipleship Resources. All rights reserved. Permission is granted to reproduce one copy of the letter for each participant.

SESSION DEVOTIONS

Session Two

Dwelling in the Word (30 minutes)

Prayer

Almighty God,
> whose Son our Savior Jesus Christ is the light of the world:
Grant that your people,
> illumined by your Word and Sacraments,
> may shine with the radiance of Christ's glory,
> that he may be known, worshiped, and obeyed
>> to the ends of the earth;
through Jesus Christ our Lord,
> who with you and the Holy Spirit lives and reigns,
> one God, now and for ever. *Amen.* (BCP, 215)

Scripture: Matthew 5:43-48

Reflection (10 minutes)

Instruct participants to partner with a person whom they do not know well.

Each person has three minutes to respond to the question, *What captured your imagination in the scripture reading?*

Listen carefully, because each person will be invited to share briefly with the group what his or her partner had to say. It is okay to take notes.

Allow six minutes for the pairs to share with each other. Signal to the group when three minutes has passed and it is time for the other person to share. At the end of the six minutes, bring the conversation to a close and invite persons to share briefly with the class what they heard their partner say.

After everyone has spoken, invite the class to discuss what God is up to in this passage for the church today.

Invite the class to respond in "popcorn" fashion. You may want to note a summary of each comment on a chalk/whiteboard.

Hymn, "O Come and Dwell in Me," *UMH*, no. 388

Copyright © 2013 by Discipleship Resources. All rights reserved. Permission is granted to reproduce one copy of this page for each participant.

Session Three

Dwelling in the Word (30 minutes)

Prayer

> O God, the strength of all who put their trust in you:
> Mercifully accept our prayers;
>> and because in our weakness we can do nothing good
>> without you,
>> give us the help of your grace,
>> that in keeping your commandments
>>> we may please you both in will and deed;
> through Jesus Christ our Lord,
>> who lives and reigns with you and the Holy Spirit,
>> one God, for ever and ever. *Amen.* (BCP, 216)

Scripture: Matthew 22:34-40

Reflection (10 minutes)

Instruct participants to partner with a person whom they do not know well.

Each person has three minutes to respond to the question, *What captured your imagination in the scripture reading?*

Listen carefully, because each person will be invited to share briefly with the group what his or her partner had to say. It is okay to take notes.

Allow six minutes for the pairs to share with each other. Signal to the group when three minutes has passed and it is time for the other person to share. At the end of the six minutes, bring the conversation to a close and invite each person to share briefly with the class what they heard their partner say.

After everyone has spoken, invite the class to discuss what God is up to in this passage for the church today.

Invite the class to respond in "popcorn" fashion. You may want to note a summary of each comment on a chalk/whiteboard.

Hymn, "Let Us Plead for Faith Alone," *UMH*, no. 385

Copyright © 2013 by Discipleship Resources. All rights reserved. Permission is granted to reproduce one copy of this page for each participant.

Session Four

Dwelling in the Word (30 minutes)

Prayer

O Lord, you have taught us
   that without love whatever we do is worth nothing:
Send your Holy Spirit and pour into our hearts your greatest
      gift,
   which is love,
   the true bond of peace and of all virtue,
      without which whoever lives is accounted dead before you.
Grant this for the sake of your only Son Jesus Christ,
   who lives and reigns with you and the Holy Spirit,
   one God, now and forever. *Amen.* (BCP, 216)

Scripture: 1 John 3:11-22

Reflection (10 minutes)

Instruct participants to partner with a person whom they do not
know well.

Each person has three minutes to respond to the question, *What
captured your imagination in the scripture reading?*

Listen carefully, because each person will be invited to share
briefly with the group what his or her partner had to say. It is okay
to take notes.

Allow six minutes for the pairs to share with each other. Signal
to the group when three minutes has passed and it is time for the
other person to share. At the end of the six minutes, bring the
conversation to a close and invite persons to share briefly with the
class what they heard their partner say.

After everyone has spoken, invite the class to discuss what God is
up to in this passage for the church today.

Invite the class to respond in "popcorn" fashion. You may want to
note a summary of each comment on a chalk/whiteboard.

Hymn, "Love Divine, All Loves Excelling," *UMH*, no. 384

**Copyright © 2013 by Discipleship Resources. All rights reserved. Permission is
granted to reproduce one copy of this page for each participant.**

Session Five

Dwelling in the Word (30 minutes)

Prayer

> O God, you have taught us to keep all your commandments
> > by loving you and our neighbor:
> Grant us the grace of your Holy Spirit,
> > that we may be devoted to you
> > > with our whole heart,
> > and united to one another with pure affection;
> through Jesus Christ our Lord,
> > who lives and reigns with you and the Holy Spirit,
> > one God, for ever and ever. *Amen.* (BCP, 230–231)

Scripture: Ephesians 4:1-16

Reflection (10 minutes)

Instruct participants to partner with a person whom they do not know well.

Each person has three minutes to respond to the question, *What captured your imagination in the scripture reading?*

Listen carefully, because each person will be invited to share briefly with the group what his or her partner had to say. It is okay to take notes.

Allow six minutes for the pairs to share with each other. Signal to the group when three minutes has passed and it is time for the other person to share. At the end of the six minutes, bring the conversation to a close and invite persons to share briefly with the class what they heard their partner say.

After everyone has spoken, invite the class to discuss what God is up to in this passage for the church today.

Invite the class to respond in "popcorn" fashion. You may want to note a summary of each comment on a chalk/whiteboard.

Hymn, "Jesus, United by Thy Grace," *UMH*, no. 561

Copyright © 2013 by Discipleship Resources. All rights reserved. Permission is granted to reproduce one copy of this page for each participant.

The Cross~Shaped Life

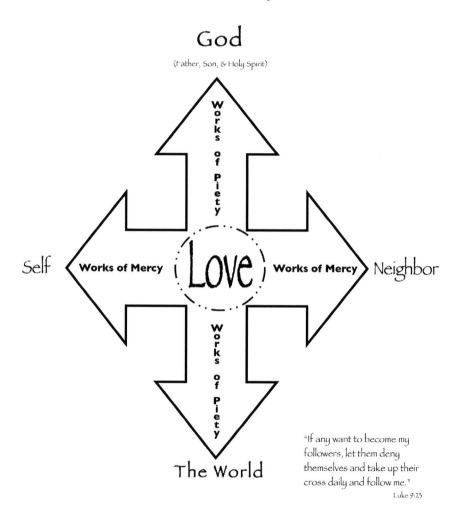

God
(Father, Son, & Holy Spirit)

Self

Neighbor

The World

"If any want to become my followers, let them deny themselves and take up their cross daily and follow me."
Luke 9:23

Copyright © 2013 by Discipleship Resources. All rights reserved. Permission is granted to reproduce one copy for each participant.

The Cross-Shaped Life:
Holiness of Heart and Life

Christians are a cross-shaped people. The cross that is represented in the diagram corresponds to the way of Jesus summarized in Luke 9:23 and the Great Commandment (Mark 12:29-31, Matt. 22:37-39, and Luke 10:25-37).

God has given us the grace and practices needed to live the way of Jesus. The vertical beam of the cross represents the divine-human relationship. The **works of piety** (prayer, worship, the Lord's Supper, scripture, listening to the Word, and fasting) are the *means of grace* God gives us to grow and mature in loving God. The horizontal beam represents the relationship between self and neighbor (those whom God loves). The **works of mercy** (acts of compassion and justice, such as feeding the hungry, welcoming strangers, caring for the sick, visiting prisoners, and witnessing for Christ) are the *means of grace* God gives to love our neighbor as ourselves and, in the process, live out our love for God in the world God loves.

At the center of the cross is love, which is the nature of God who is Father, Son, and Holy Spirit. It is this love that makes the cross-shaped life possible.

The cross-shaped life is surrounded by **grace**. Grace is prevenient (preparing), justifying (restoring), and sanctifying (sustaining). It brings us to Jesus and empowers us to respond to his love by living his way in the world. As we live his way he opens our hearts and minds to grace. We experience this grace according to where we are in relation to Christ and our neighbors. The **works of piety** (acts of worship and devotion) and **works of mercy** (acts of compassion and justice) are the holy habits through which God conveys grace into our lives. In turn, we become channels of grace for the world.

The vertical dimension of cross-shaped discipleship is summarized in Mark 12:29-30. The horizontal dimension is summarized in Mark 12:31.

Jesus tells the people about the cost of following him in Luke 9:23. The cross Jesus calls his disciples to take up is obedience to his teachings summarized in the Great Commandment.

The apostle Paul describes the nature and outcome of discipleship in Galatians 5:6, 22-23. The nature is "faith working by love" and the outcome is holiness of heart and life. These marks of holiness are what Paul calls the "fruit of the Spirit" and John Wesley calls the "holy tempers." When Christians surrender to living the way of Jesus, grace sets them free to fully become the persons God created them to be. Their character becomes a reflection of the character of Jesus Christ.

The General Rule of Discipleship

Two Great Commandments

When asked what is the greatest commandment Jesus summarizes his teachings in two commandments, "'You shall love the Lord your God with all your heart, and with all your soul, and with all your mind.' This is the greatest and first commandment. And a second is like it: 'You shall love your neighbor as yourself.' On these two commandments hang all the law and the prophets" (Matt. 22:37-40).

In Covenant Discipleship groups, these two great commandments are applied through a General Rule of Discipleship that shapes their life and work:

The General Rule of Discipleship

To witness to Jesus Christ in the world and to follow his teachings through acts of compassion, justice, worship, and devotion under the guidance of the Holy Spirit.

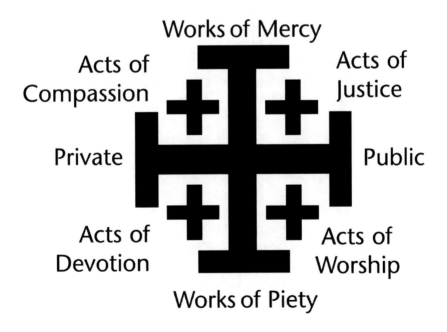

Works of Mercy

Acts of Compassion — Acts of Justice

Private — Public

Acts of Devotion — Acts of Worship

Works of Piety

The United Methodist Rule of Life

The following excerpt is from *The Book of Discipline of The United Methodist Church* ¶ 104.

The Nature, Design, and General Rules of Our United Societies

In the latter end of the year 1739 eight or ten persons came to Mr. Wesley, in London, who appeared to be deeply convinced of sin, and earnestly groaning for redemption. They desired, as did two or three more the next day, that he would spend some time with them in prayer, and advise them how to flee from the wrath to come, which they saw continually hanging over their heads. That he might have more time for this great work, he appointed a day when they might all come together, which from thenceforward they did every week, namely, on Thursday in the evening. To these, and as many more as desired to join with them (for their number increased daily), he gave those advices from time to time which he judged most needful for them, and they always concluded their meeting with prayer suited to their several necessities.

This was the rise of the **United Society**, first in Europe, and then in America. Such a society is no other than "a company of men having the *form* and seeking the *power* of godliness, united in order to pray together, to receive the word of exhortation, and to watch over one another in love, that they may help each other to work out their salvation."

That it may the more easily be discerned whether they are indeed working out their own salvation, each society is divided into smaller companies, called **classes**, according to their respective places of abode. There are about twelve persons in a class, one of whom is styled the **leader**. It is his duty:

1. To see each person in his class once a week at least, in order:

- to inquire how their souls prosper;
- to advise, reprove, comfort or exhort, as occasion may require;
- to receive what they are willing to give toward the relief of the preachers, church, and poor.

2. To meet the ministers and the stewards of the society once a week, in order:

- to inform the minister of any that are sick, or of any that walk disorderly and will not be reproved;
- to pay the stewards what they have received of their several classes in the week preceding.

There is only one condition previously required of those who desire admission into these societies: "a desire to flee from the wrath to come, and to be saved from their sins." But wherever this is really fixed in the soul it will be shown by its fruits.

It is therefore expected of all who continue therein that they should continue to evidence their desire of salvation,

First: By doing no harm, by avoiding evil of every kind, especially that which is most generally practiced, such as:

- The taking of the name of God in vain.
- The profaning the day of the Lord, either by doing ordinary work therein or by buying or selling.
- Drunkenness: buying or selling spirituous liquors, or drinking them, unless in cases of extreme necessity.
- Slaveholding; buying or selling slaves.
- Fighting, quarreling, brawling, brother going to law with brother; returning evil for evil, or railing for railing; the using many words in buying or selling.
- The buying or selling goods that have not paid the duty.
- The giving or taking things on usury—i.e., unlawful interest.
- Uncharitable or unprofitable conversation; particularly speaking evil of magistrates or of ministers.
- Doing to others as we would not they should do unto us.
- Doing what we know is not for the glory of God, as:
  - The putting on of gold and costly apparel.
  - The taking such diversions as cannot be used in the name of the Lord Jesus.
  - The singing those songs, or reading those books, which do not tend to the knowledge or love of God.

- ◆ Softness and needless self-indulgence.
- ◆ Laying up treasure upon earth.
- ◆ Borrowing without a probability of paying; or taking up goods without a probability of paying for them.

It is expected of all who continue in these societies that they should continue to evidence their desire of salvation,

Secondly: By doing good; by being in every kind merciful after their power; as they have opportunity, doing good of every possible sort, and, as far as possible, to all men:

To their bodies, of the ability which God giveth, by giving food to the hungry, by clothing the naked, by visiting or helping them that are sick or in prison.

To their souls, by instructing, reproving, or exhorting all we have any intercourse with; trampling under foot that enthusiastic doctrine that "we are not to do good unless *our hearts be free to it*."

By doing good, especially to them that are of the household of faith or groaning so to be; employing them preferably to others; buying one of another, helping each other in business, and so much the more because the world will love its own and them only.

By all possible diligence and frugality, that the gospel be not blamed.

By running with patience the race which is set before them, denying themselves, and taking up their cross daily; submitting to bear the reproach of Christ, to be as the filth and offscouring of the world; and looking that men should say all manner of evil of them *falsely*, for the Lord's sake.

It is expected of all who desire to continue in these societies that they should continue to evidence their desire of salvation,

Thirdly: By attending upon all the ordinances of God; such are:

- • The public worship of God.
- • The ministry of the Word, either read or expounded.
- • The Supper of the Lord.
- • Family and private prayer.
- • Searching the Scriptures.
- • Fasting or abstinence.

These are the General Rules of our societies; all of which we are taught of God to observe, even in his written Word, which is the only rule, and the sufficient rule, both of our faith and practice. And all these we know his Spirit writes on truly awakened hearts. If there be any among us who observe them not, who habitually break any of them, let it be known unto them who watch over that soul as they who must give an account. We will admonish him of the error of his ways. We will bear with him for a season. But then, if he repent not, he hath no more place among us. We have delivered our own souls.

A Sample Covenant

In gratitude for the grace of Jesus Christ, in whose death we have died and in whose resurrection we have found new life, we pledge to be his disciples. We recognize that our time and talents are gifts from God, and we will use them to search out God's will for us and to obey. We will do our best not to compromise the will of God for human goals. We will serve both God and his creation earnestly and lovingly. We respect and accept fully all group members, whose integrity and confidentiality we will uphold in all that we share. With God's grace we make our covenant.

> I* will spend four hours each month helping the poor people in my community.
>
> When I am aware of injustice to others, I will not remain silent.
>
> I will obey the promptings of the Holy Spirit to serve God and my neighbor.
>
> I will heed the warnings of the Holy Spirit not to sin against God and my neighbor.
>
> I will worship each Sunday, unless prevented.
>
> I will receive the sacrament of Holy Communion each week.
>
> I will pray each day, privately and with family or friends.
>
> I will read and study the Scriptures each day.
>
> I will return to Christ the first tenth of all I receive.
>
> I will prayerfully care for my body and for the world in which I live.

I hereby make my commitment, trusting in the grace of God to give me the will and the strength to keep this covenant.

Date: _____ Signed: _____

* The use of the personal "I" or the collective "We" is entirely at the discretion of each group.

Copyright © 2013 by Discipleship Resources. All rights reserved. Permission is granted to reproduce one copy of this page for each participant.

Means of Grace

"By 'means of grace' I understand outward signs, words, or actions ordained of God, and appointed for this end—to be the ordinary channels whereby he might convey to men & women preventing, justifying, or sanctifying grace" (John Wesley, Sermon 16: "The Means of Grace").

The General Rule of Discipleship

To witness to Jesus Christ in the world and to follow his teachings through acts of compassion, justice, worship, and devotion under the guidance of the Holy Spirit.

The Works of Mercy

"You shall love your neighbor as yourself" (Matthew 22:39)
- By doing no harm, by avoiding evil of every kind, especially that which is most generally practiced
- By doing good; by being in every kind merciful after their power . . . doing good of every possible sort, and as far as possible, to all people. . .
- Giving food to the hungry
- Clothing the naked
- Visiting or helping them that are sick or in prison
- Instructing, reproving, or exhorting all with the good news of Jesus Christ
- Acts of Compassion and Acts of Justice

The Works of Piety

"You shall love the Lord your God with all your heart, and with all your soul, and with all your mind" (Matthew 22:37)
- By attending upon all the ordinances of God
- The public worship of God
- The ministry of the Word, either read or expounded
- The Supper of the Lord
- Family and private prayer
- Searching the Scriptures
- Fasting or abstinence
- Acts of Worship and Acts of Devotion

The United Methodist Church
Job Description Form

Job title: *Disciple of Jesus Christ*

Work location:

Reports to:

_____ **Full-time**

_____ **Part-time**

Essential Duties and Responsibilities:

Education and/or Work Experience Requirements:

Physical Requirements:

Print Employee Name

Employee Signature   **Date**